Hidden Under Water

Hidden Under Water

Kim Taylor

Delacorte Press

Published by Delacorte Press
Bantam Doubleday Dell Publishing Group, Inc.
666 Fifth Avenue, New York, New York 10103
This work was first published in Great Britain
in 1990 by Belitha Press Limited.
Text copyright © Kim Taylor 1990
Photographs copyright © Kim Taylor and
Jane Burton 1990
Consultant: Ellen Fader

Manufactured in Great Britain
September 1990
10 9 8 7 6 5 4 3 2 1

Library of Congress Cataloguing-in-Publication
Data will be printed in subsequent editions.
ISBN 0-385-30184-7
ISBN 0-385-30185-5 (lib. bdg.)

*U*NLESS YOU ARE LUCKY ENOUGH TO GO DIVING, YOU cannot enjoy the fascinating world at the bottom of a dark pond or in the depths of the ocean. Even when diving, you can stay only for a little while. But the underwater world is the home of many different kinds of animals. Some of them breathe water, and others breathe air.

The European pond turtle (*opposite*) spends about half its life out of water and has feet for walking on land. But the hawksbill turtle (*above*) spends almost all of its life in the sea and has flippers for swimming. Both are reptiles and breathe air.

Taking a breath

WHEN YOU LOOK ACROSS A POND, THE SURFACE OF the water is like a mirror. You cannot see *into* the pond; you can only see a reflection of what is above it. But when a terrapin (*above left*) or a caiman (*above right*) comes up to breathe, you can see its head clearly, together with its upside-down reflection. The Malayan mud turtle (*opposite*) does not need to put its whole head out of water to breathe. It stays buried in the mud of its shallow stream and just breaks the water surface with the tip of its long, thin snout.

From water to land

SOME ANIMALS SPEND PART OF THEIR LIVES IN WATER. These frog tadpoles (*below left*) hatch from the spawn as little round bodies with long tails and gills with which to breathe water. But you can see that one of the tadpoles is already starting to grow a thin leg. The tadpoles feed by scraping plants with their mouths. As the tadpoles get bigger, their legs get stronger, but they still only have hind legs (*below right*).

Soon the tadpoles start to sprout front legs as well. Here is one tadpole with four legs and one with still only two (*below left*). Both tadpoles have long tails for swimming. At this stage they start to breathe air, swimming to the surface of their pond now and again to take a mouthful. When their legs are strong enough, the tadpoles climb out of the water. Their tails are slowly taken back into their bodies, and they become little frogs (*below right*) that can live on land as well as in water.

Colored coral

*T*HE PIECES OF HARD WHITE CORAL THAT YOU FIND washed up on the beaches of warm countries are really the skeletons of soft undersea animals. Under-water, a living coral is often brightly colored. It has lots of soft heads called *polyps*, each surrounded by ten-tacles. When the polyps are disturbed, they retract into their hard skeleton. You can see this happening in the picture (*opposite*). The polyps disappear when a pair of prawns walk over the coral. The two corals (*below*), like all corals, breathe water through their skins and extract from the sea water material to build their stony skeletons.

Flowers and featherdusters

*T*HE BEAUTIFUL SEA ANEMONE LOOKS LIKE CORAL, BUT it doesn't have a skeleton. Anemones feed on small animals that accidentally swim near them. Tiny stinging cells on the tentacles shoot poison into any little fish that touches them, and then the tentacles curl around the fish so that it cannot swim away. The spider crab (*above right*) is gently exploring the anemone to see if it can steal its dinner. The crab will not be caught because it is too clever.

Fanworms live in tubes and feed by filtering little bits of food out of sea water. To do this, they have big fans around their mouths. As they drift along in the water, any food particles that touch a fan are carried down its arms to the mouth of the worm—like people being carried down an escalator. The featherduster worm (*above left*) is a fanworm with an especially large fan. This featherduster (*above right*) has smaller fanworms of a different sort living underneath it. All fanworms are very sensitive and they disappear quickly into their tubes if they are disturbed.

Beautiful fishes

*I*N THE WATER AROUND A CORAL REEF, THERE ARE thousands of fishes. Many of them are beautifully colored like the royal gramma (*above left*) and the electric-blue damselfish (*above right*). Bright colors are all right for little coral fish because they can escape from big fish by darting into one of the hundreds of cracks and crannies in the reef. Where there is no coral, little fishes must hide their colors, like the corkwing wrasse (*opposite*), whose blue is in stripes to match the seaweed.

Hidden fishes

*F*ISHES THAT LIVE ON THE BOTTOM OF STREAMS LIKE these catfish (*above left*) have to match the color of the stones, otherwise a hungry heron may spot them. In the sea, the lumpsucker (*above right*) matches both the color and the shape of the seaweed bladder it is sitting on. Its fins underneath are joined together to form a sucker so that it can stick onto the weed. Both catfish and lumpsuckers are slow swimmers and cannot escape from big fish. They rely on their colors to hide them.

Many fishes that swim in the open sea have silver scales on their sides, like these mojarras (*above left*). You might think that the shiny silver would make the fish easy to see. When you shine a light directly on them from the side—as has been done here—they *do* indeed show up brightly. But at sea, the silver sides of the fish are like mirrors and reflect the deep blue of the water around them, making them almost invisible. The baby flounder (*above right*) is difficult to see because its body is nearly transparent.

Eight arms

SQUIDS ARE SOME OF THE CLEVEREST ANIMALS IN THE sea. They have very good eyesight. They can swim fast—frontward *or* backward. They can change color very quickly and, when chased by a fish, they can squirt out a blob of black ink that disguises them and fools the fish. This squid (*above*) is hanging in the water with its eight arms curled over its head. It will dart off by jetting water out of the little tube beneath its head. An octopus (*opposite*) also has eight arms and huge bright eyes, but spends its life at the bottom of the sea. It hunts among the rocks, trapping its victims with the suckers that cover its rubbery arms.

Tight skins

LOBSTERS AND CRABS DON'T HAVE A SKELETON INSIDE their bodies. Instead, they have a hard skin that does not stretch—so how can they grow? They have to throw off their old skin and grow a new one. The Pacific lobster (*above*) has just sloughed its old skin. The new skin underneath is soft and more brightly colored than the old. This soft skin can stretch quite a lot before it hardens. The hermit crab (*opposite*) had to come out of its shell for a few seconds to slough off its skin.

Underwater surprises

*I*F YOU WERE A BIRD FLYING OVER THE SEA, YOU MIGHT be surprised if a fish flew past you! But flying fish (*above*) are common in many warm seas. Their fins are huge and the bottom half of their tail is long. They use their tails to drive themselves over the surface until they have enough speed to glide for long distances on out-stretched fins. They sometimes land unexpectedly on the decks of ships.

If you were a fish in a pond, you would be equally surprised to meet a furry water shrew—its coat silver with trapped air bubbles (*opposite*)—swimming past.

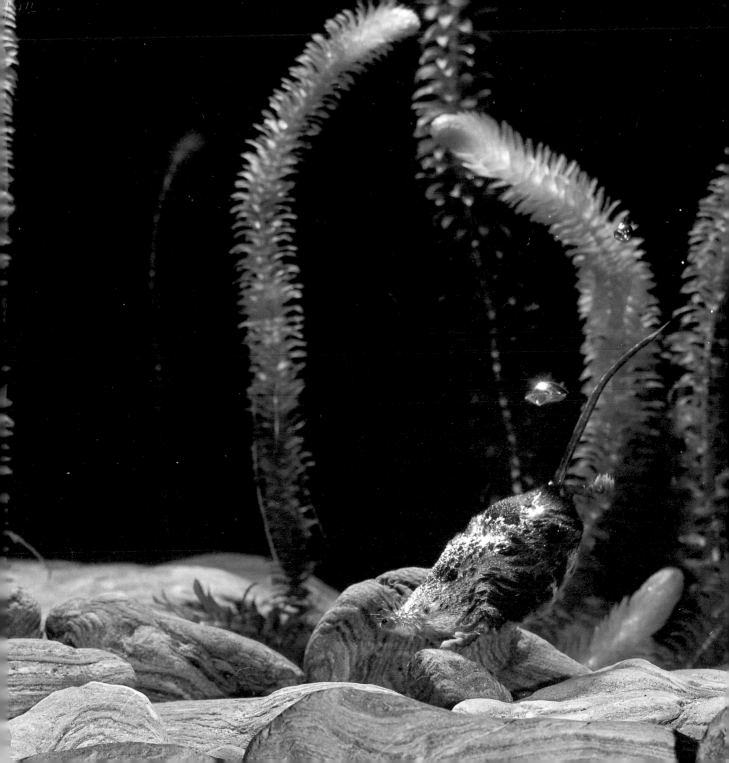

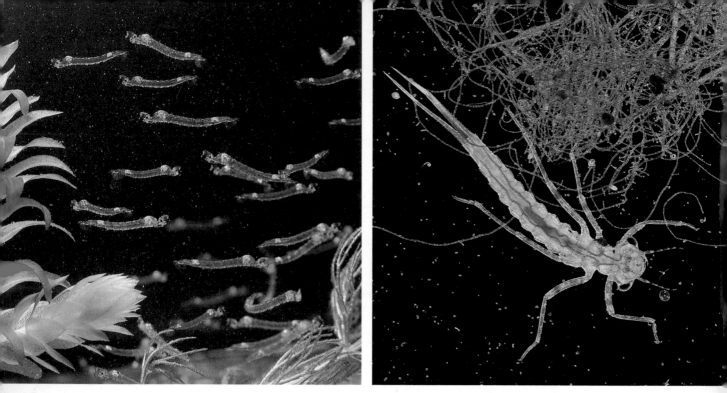

Water nymphs

MANY INSECTS SPEND MUCH OF THEIR LIVES AS nymphs or larvae in ponds and rivers. They do most of their feeding and all of their growing in the water. These phantom midge larvae (*above left*) are transparent and have little bubbles at each end. They float in the water and use the hook on their heads to catch water fleas. Damselfly nymphs can be brown or a beautiful green like this one (*above right*). They creep slowly through the water weed looking for moving prey. In early summer, they climb out of the water and hatch into lovely damselflies with shimmering wings.

Black fly larvae attach themselves to weeds and stones in fast-running streams. They have fan-shaped arms to filter food out of the water. When the larvae are full grown, they stick themselves down firmly and turn into pupae, like these on a water plant leaf (*below left*). They breathe water through trailing gills. In spring the tiny black flies hatch out and climb up through the water to dry their wings before flying off (*below right*). They are also known as buffalo gnats and sometimes drive people and animals crazy with their bites.

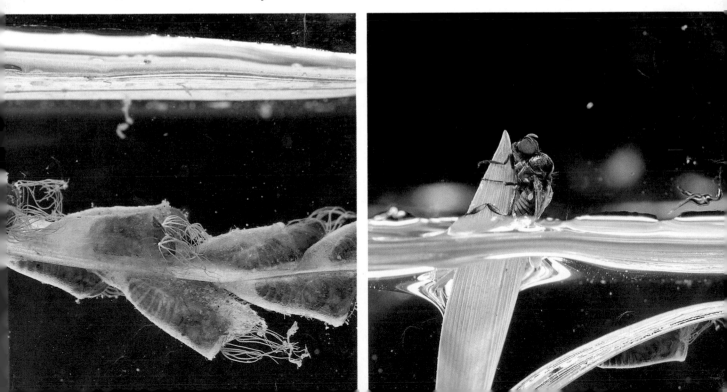

Ride a Sea Horse

A SEA HORSE IS A VERY STRANGE KIND OF FISH. IT SWIMS along in an upright position, holding its long-nosed head up, rather like a horse. It doesn't wave its tail to swim like other fishes, but waves the fin on its back instead. Its long thin tail has no fin and can be curled around seaweed as an anchor. The male sea horse has a special pouch for carrying eggs that have been laid by the female. When the eggs hatch and all the little sea horses swim out, it is just as if the father is giving birth!

Index